# Renewal

## 31 DAY DEVOTIONAL STORIES, PRAYERS AND PROMISES

FRED CARLSON

WESTBOW
PRESS*
A DIVISION OF THOMAS NELSON
& ZONDERVAN

This book is a work of non-fiction. Unless otherwise noted, the author and the publisher make no explicit guarantees as to the accuracy of the information contained in this book and in some cases, names of people and places have been altered to protect their privacy.

WestBow Press books may be ordered through booksellers or by contacting:

WestBow Press
A Division of Thomas Nelson & Zondervan
1663 Liberty Drive
Bloomington, IN 47403
www.westbowpress.com
844-714-3454

Because of the dynamic nature of the Internet, any web addresses or links contained in this book may have changed since publication and may no longer be valid. The views expressed in this work are solely those of the author and do not necessarily reflect the views of the publisher, and the publisher hereby disclaims any responsibility for them.

Any people depicted in stock imagery provided by Getty Images are models, and such images are being used for illustrative purposes only. Certain stock imagery © Getty Images.

ISBN: 978-1-6642-4500-6 (sc)
ISBN: 978-1-6642-4501-3 (hc)
ISBN: 978-1-6642-4499-3 (e)

Library of Congress Control Number: 2021918903

Print information available on the last page.

WestBow Press rev. date: 09/30/2021

# Dedication

This book is dedicated to the efforts of three faith-based organizations, whose purpose is to nurture the spiritual health of men, women and families, broken and wounded by addiction.

**Calvary Mission:**
Community ministry; Upper Kalskag, Alaska

**Changing Gaits:**
Equine-assisted recovery therapy for men; Brook Park, Minnesota

**Dunklin Memorial Camp:**
Recovery and skills training for men and women in Okeechobee, Florida

# Introduction

I had passed by the small flower earlier without giving it much notice. But now the day was far spent, and the setting sun was resting low on the soft, saltwater horizon. Brilliant beams of backlight came streaming through its fragile translucent petals. The resolute light gave voice to the flower: *"I'll not remain silent; I have much to say."* I listened, feeling both admonished and privileged at the same moment. Once again, the Holy Spirit was graciously attempting to enter my consciousness. I was given a vivid awareness of His presence and purpose. The *eternal* stepped into my *temporal* physical world to rescue me from nearsightedness. My soul opened to the warmth of His companionship as He spoke to my heart: *I send signs and symbols of light into your life to capture your attention; I desire more for you. I care about how you spend your days. Your walk and attitude are prone to missing out on the greatest gifts I've provided for you. Listen and respond to the call of my voice, lest you abandon the many blessings of my great and precious promises. (Inspired by 2 Peter 1:1-10)*

Life is a continuous contest between the temporal and the eternal. Man naturally loves to trust in science, numbers and technology. We are indeed data-driven and generally proud of it. Information has become our security blanket of choice, but *data* has no love for mankind. Lasting contentment comes only through prayerful communion with God.

*"Prayer is a pasturage, a field, wherein all the virtues
find their nourishment, growth, and strength."*
Catherine of Siena, 1347

For each of us there is deep inside, a loving voice, competing for our attention. When we pause to listen intently and singularly to that one voice, we enter into a greater reality. It is a sacred place where lasting encouragement waits for us, dispelling fear, and literally grasping our hearts, defeating the mediocrity, burdens, and dooming pressures of the hour.

I urge the reader to make the reading of this devotional a 31-day consistent exercise. Don't read ahead, but rather reserve time to prayerfully ponder the daily challenge, "Today in-Christ." As you taste and savor the scriptures, your personal benefit will blossom.

You will notice I often use the term "*in-Christ*." The meaning may be found in Psalms:

> *He who dwells in the secret place of the Most High
> shall remain stable and fixed under the shadow of
> the Almighty [Whose power no foe can withstand].
> I will say of the Lord, He is my Refuge and my
> Fortress, my God; on Him I lean and rely, and in
> Him I [confidently] trust! Psalms 91:1-2 AMPC*

To live *in-Christ* is to consciously, deliberately, desire the presence of the Holy Spirit. It can be likened to opening a door and walking into a new dwelling place. This is indeed *the secret place within the heart* where only you and the Holy Spirit can go. In this place, God speaks and brings profound healing and strength. It is a place of *refuge*; it is a *fortress* from which we can confidently fight our battles.

*Strangler Fig overtaking a Cypress, Fakahatchee*
*Strand Preserve, Everglades, Florida*

## 1

# Recovery

When I first saw the afflicted tree, I felt a sad realization. The mighty Pond Cypress can live to be more than 2,000 years old, but the life in this century-old tree was gone, severely cut short. I was reminded of that chapter in my life when my faith was temporarily suffocated.

**Isaiah 42:3a (NIV)**
*A bruised reed he will not break, and a smoldering wick he will not snuff out.*

Before entering the University, I had a daily, conversational relationship with the Holy Spirit. But as I became part of the university community, I felt an unspoken mandate to become so *open-minded,* that I questioned all my conservative Christian convictions and values. I stopped reading my Bible and soon abandoned prayer as well. After a couple months, I was miserable. Jesus Christ, my closest, forever-friend, seemed very distant.

It was fall and I went on a quick hunting trip to Montana with several of my brothers. It was good to be with them. I came to terms with *life* again, as the Holy Spirit tugged at my conscience. Late one night, I lay awake on the prairie under the stars and knew I needed to reconcile my heart with my Heavenly Father. It was well after midnight when I got out of the sack and walked into the cold night air. I told the Lord how sorry I was and how much I missed Him. Suddenly, His presence was there. I fell first to my knees, and then forward, face-down. I had no choice. I knew it was His way of emphatically saying, "*I Am* and *I love you.*" My joy returned!

Repentance, reconciliation and recovery are like three brothers, united via the heart. They walk, work and live together. *Recovery* is the heart's response to the universal illness of pride and selfishness. Some spiritual illnesses are more apparent than others – but they all attempt to suffocate one's faith. Addiction has many faces, and all are potentially deadly. Discouragement, busyness, doubts, and stifling fear all have the capacity to steal our peace and readiness to care for ourselves and others.

### Romans 6:6 (NIV)
*For we know that our old self was crucified with him so that the body ruled by sin might be done away with, that we should no longer be slaves to sin.*

*"Resolve to live in Christ."* What does this really mean? Our bent toward hardness of heart is strong, as we have all tasted of its

debilitating tyranny. Humanity is by nature idolatrous. Too quickly and too often we entrust our keeping to *self*, rather than to Jesus Christ. Can I actually take captive my attitudes, checking motives and intentions before I act or speak? When I selfishly choose to run ahead of, or away from God, will He slow my pace and show me the futile, rabbit trails of my own making ... if I ask Him to do so? Will the fruits of His Spirit begin to more naturally manifest themselves in me? Is it possible to live joyfully in the midst of continuing conflict? Will I learn to recognize His voice when He speaks in a whisper, amidst the noise of many selfish voices?

We can wholeheartedly answer these questions with an emphatic, *"Yes!"* When people first become free *in Christ*, they often move forward with a boldness that causes others to desire that same faith. The clarity of their conviction is generally not the result of deep theological study; it is singularly the result of God's forgiveness in response to the sinner's remorse for his sin. Jesus Christ hears the desperate cry of a heart once hardened or blind. He steps into the suffocating battle and says, *"Forgiven, follow me."*

### Galatians 5:1 (AMP)
*In [this] freedom Christ has made us free [and completely liberated us]; stand fast then, and do not be hampered and held ensnared and submit again to a yoke of slavery [which you have once put off].*

### Time Out
Precious Father, today I want to align my will with Yours. Lord, please continue to inspire Christian people across our nation and in our neighborhoods to step forward as servants to mentor, encourage and care for the brokenhearted. May we who are wounded and discouraged come to know, love, follow and enjoy You forever. Amen.

**Today in-Christ**
I will pray for one specific, struggling individual, that God will open their spiritual eyes, soften and encourage their heart, and lead them into a transformational faith-relationship with Christ. I'll prayerfully consider the likelihood that God may want me to personally stand and walk with this person.

**Recovery**
Remove the walls, self-centered reasons …
They hinder my walk and block my sight.
I choose to seek Him in all seasons
I resolve to live in Christ.

May I hear God's call and follow close
Resist the lie; embrace the pain
Stand strong and trust
In Jesus' name.

*Near Jekyll Island, Georgia*

## 2

# *Crossing Over*

Not all bridges serve an obvious, fruitful purpose. I once traveled for more than an hour on a small state forest road of Louisiana. Curiosity was my only motivation. The road kept getting smaller until it disappeared completely into the brush. On foot, I walked beyond and discovered a very substantial bridge over a river! It had long been blocked by a pile of dirt, now overgrown thick with brush. The bridge was heavily constructed – a massive amount of concrete. Apparently, this bridge was a mistake – and had never served a purpose.

Some of our own mistakes have also been months – or even years – in the making. As I contemplated the scene, I was moved to consider its symbolic value; the fickleness of some of my own life-pursuits. Some efforts – which seemed so justified and necessary at the time – were later abandoned in the wake of other seemingly imperative tasks. So it is with many of the pursuits of mankind. When we finally pause to look back and ponder, we may see bridges that go nowhere – if we can see them at all.

Thankfully, I encountered the most precious bridge of all time when I was 10 years old. It was a June summer day, and there had been serious tension in my family. I desired so much for my beloved Mom and Dad and six brothers to all get along with each other. I wanted to escape from the fighting, so I walked to the end of our farm driveway. I stopped and looked back at our beautiful farm. My brother Martin was mowing hay and the smell of red clover permeated the air. I imagined heaven might smell like that. Then in that despairing moment, the Holy Spirit became vividly real to me, initiating a life-long connection that transported me to a better place. In Vacation Bible School, I'd learned of a Heavenly Father; but, until that instant, I hadn't crossed over. I felt the warmth of His Presence, and so I prayed, asking God to help me understand my family and to bring me more of the hope and joy I felt that very moment. The Holy Spirit's presence immediately bathed me in a rich, new confidence. I received from Him a simple yet profound message: *"Everything will be OK."*

### Isaiah 51:10 (NIV)
*Was it not you who dried up the sea, the waters of the great deep, who made a road in the depths of the sea so that the redeemed might cross over?*

I returned home eager to share the good news with my Mom. She was hanging up clothes in the backyard. I told her God had spoken to me. She knelt to eye-level and in earnest asked, *"What did He say?"* I answered, *"God said everything is going to be okay."* Mom appeared to be greatly encouraged, and my faith was affirmed.

## Time Out
Precious Father, I praise You for making a *way* that I may cross over from despair and fear, to hope. Thank You for Your mercy and kindness. Forgive me for those times when I have squandered Your grace. Still, Your love endures. You remain faithful even when I am not. Amen.

## Today in-Christ
I'll confess the burdens of my heart to my Heavenly Father and ask him for the faith to know that *in-Christ,* everything will be OK.

## Ephesians 1:17 (NIV)
*I keep asking that the God of our Lord Jesus Christ, the glorious Father, may give you the Spirit of wisdom and revelation, so that you may know him better.*

## Crossing Over
A precious bridge
Your outstretched arms
Hold back the waters
And calm the sea
By faith we cross over –
All this for me.

*Snake River Valley, Minnesota*

## 3

# Radical Light

Returning home from a canoe trip with a group of thirty young adults, I was hit with a sudden sadness. Our camping experience in the Superior National Forest had been a success. The Spirit's presence was powerfully realized in our large and small group sessions. We had grown in our understanding of God's love and of life principles. I was confident the core-heart of the group had been positively impacted. Yet, when we were about ten miles from home, an outspoken, negative doubt rushed over me: *Has anything really changed? Will these youth be better prepared to make healthy, life-choices? On Monday morning will we slip back into our previous selfish attitudes?*

Just then the old blue van crested over the hill above the Snake River valley. The June setting sun hit the power lines. They glistened from pole to pole, descending into the valley and beyond. This visual became God's response, my defense against the destroyer of joy, Satan. The light hitting the lines was like musical refrains of an old hymn; the Father was making His message abundantly clear.

Light is a dynamic change-agent. When even a single ray touches anything, it makes a dramatic difference; often creating a radical transformation. The ordinary becomes extraordinary. The landscape we thought mundane, suddenly flashes its eyes in a new, brilliant way. Such is the work of the Holy Spirit. Our hope is in Him.

**Time Out**
Precious Father, illumine the dark and discouraging spaces of my life that stir me to unhealthy anxiety or pride. Cast Your light on my path, that I may be established in a constructive attitude, guided by Your watch-care. Amen.

**Today in-Christ**
Today I'll not let fear or pride hinder my prayers, or let my past define who I am. *In-Christ,* I will not fall prey to discouraging voices. Help me, Father, to seek greater light and understanding.

*Philippians 1:6 (AMP)*
*And I am convinced and sure of this very thing, that He Who began a good work in you will continue until the day of Jesus Christ [right up to the time of His return], developing [that good work] and perfecting and bringing it to full completion in you.*

**Radical Light**

Within the murky grey
Of my downcast soul
A brilliant strand of gold
A declaration so bold
Pierces the darkness
Sad shadows flee
My hope returns
Running to me
All my discouragement
Heaped up in the night
Melts away in the glow
Of victorious Light.

*Alley Spring. Near Eminence, Missouri*

## 4

# History Tells

Nestled patiently between two ridges in the Ozark Mountains, Alley Spring is a quiet, peaceful place. Only the gristmill and a small church remain – the signature of departed days. Like so many others, this old mill once breathed life into an entire town: a general store, schoolhouse, shops, post office and church. I could easily imagine a day when families came with teams and wagons to grind oats and corn, the younger children running, quickly seeking out friends to play *Hide'n seek*, *Anti-I-Over* and *Captain May I*. While big brother watered the team of horses, mom and dad traded canned goods and neighborhood news with friends.

I visited for a while among this long-departed, phantom community, secretly intrigued with their lighthearted, serious, and even intimate conversations. I was amused at their levity and nearly joined in their laughter. Then in a moment, I felt I had intruded. I reluctantly stepped back into the present.

Alley Spring was once a vibrant, closely-knit town, everyone dependent in some way on the mill. So much had changed, and yet so little. Man's technology is always passing – chased off the stage by the new. Yet, without the generosity of the spring itself, there would never have been a town. Even now, millions of gallons of jade-colored water gush out of the mill-pond each day creating a literal river. That is what powered the mill. The source of that power remains today, while most of the relics of man have vanished from the scene. Now, only an occasional visitor comes to gaze with wonder into the blue-green, spring water.

**Time Out**
Precious Father, my earth-bound pursuits are temporal and fragile. Generations soon pass on, but Your life-giving Spirit remains faithful. May I not look for consolation in the conventions of man, but rather seek to intimately know You – the true source of eternal hope and goodness. Amen.

**Today in-Christ**
I will take a brief *time-out* today and contemplate God's purpose for my life. I will ask Him to speak while I listen.

**Ephesians 3:17b, 18 (NIV)**
*And I pray that you, being rooted and established in love, may have power, together with all the saints, to grasp how wide and long and high and deep is the love of Christ.*

**History Tells**

Quiet now, the mill stands still
No wheel powers her iron shaft
That once turned belts and gears
And years of progress.

*Progress to what,* I ask.

I'll listen deep and listen well
For truth is all that history tells.
It never lies but softly poses
*Is the present worth the past?*

Inventions proud but soon discarded
So we move from age to age.
Distracted from God's gifts imparted
Facing death with desperate gaze.

*Bell Tower*

## 5

# *Love Triumphs*

Directly ahead, the full, evening moon was perfectly framed within the bell tower of the old schoolhouse. As I stepped out of my car onto the deserted tar road to capture the scene, the chill in the clear, late-night air admonished me to ponder the full message of the moment. How symbolic – a heavenly light, occupying that privileged place!

When driving the country roads, which I often do, I'm always pleased to see the evidence of township government – small government, close to home. I think that's the best kind. Occasionally a small rural church will adopt as its worship place a vacant town hall – an admirable example of recycling and progress at its best. When church or town neighbors truly love and care for each other, they don't need a host of other social services. Everyone benefits. *God smiles.*

Government is about what we *do.* Our Father is concerned about who we *are.* The internal determines the external. If the grassroots people of America want the light and love of God to counsel their lives, then it's fair that we begin by disciplining our own selfish attitudes. Am I sincerely seeking a right and intimate relationship with Christ? Repentance brings forgiveness, and forgiveness delivers healing and goodwill. Where Christ's character of love and His standard of love and service to neighbor prevails, there is little need for greater government. Indeed, this was the plan of the early church.

**Time Out**
Precious Father, shine Your love and mercy into our communities. May we aggressively seek to know you and be empowered by Your grace. May we take greater personal responsibility to ease the heartache next door. Amen.

**Today in-Christ**
This week I will devote at least 15 minutes of my devotional time every morning to seeking how to follow more closely Christ's example of brotherly love. I'll ask for specific insight as to how I may become a better neighbor.

**Galatians 5:13-15 (NIV)**
*The entire law is summed up in a single command:*
*"Love your neighbor as yourself."*

**Love Triumphs**
The moon came to visit
In the old bell tower
Bearing witness to Love
Over laws of the hour.

She said with much passion,
*Don't give up the fight*
*Christ in you triumphs!*
Then moved on in the night.

*Haleakalā Volcano, Maui*

# 6

# Civil War Within

Wind, water, fire, and pressure; these metamorphic forces conspire to shape life as we know it. When one of these powers engages in hazardous behavior, a natural disaster often results. Volcanic eruptions, hurricanes, drought, floods, earthquakes, extreme heat and cold – these are the forces that build, form, and destroy. Oh, so awesome, oh, so dreadful!

Our daily lives carry within them this same perilous dichotomy – this same two-natured potential for both beauty and disaster. *Excessive self* screams for attention at my weakest moments. I can consciously attempt to wrestle my pride and self-interest to the ground; but, in my own strength I often lose the match. Only when I humbly submit to Christ's Spirit, am I able to achieve peace and hope.

### Romans 6:11-12 (AMPC)

*Even so consider yourselves also dead to sin and your relation to it broken, but alive to God [living in unbroken fellowship with Him] in Christ Jesus. Let not sin therefore rule as king in your mortal (short-lived, perishable) bodies, to make you yield to its cravings and be subject to its lusts and evil passions.*

Faith walks ahead and joy soon comes running to catch up. My joy always follows my surrender and dependence upon Christ.

### Time Out

Precious Father, each new morning Your Spirit taps me on the shoulder and asks, *Do you desire to know me better today?* Father, help me always to answer with a resounding, *Yes!* Only as I trust in You day-by-day, am I able to kill the idolatry and pride in my life. Thy will be done. I praise You, Lord Jesus. Amen.

### Today in-Christ

Today I will set aside ego and self-pity, and prayerfully enter into a conversation with the Father. I will ask for greater faith, and trust Him to open my spiritual eyes.

### Galatians 5:16 (AMP)

*But I say, walk and live [habitually] in the [Holy] Spirit [responsive to and controlled and guided by the Spirit]; then you will certainly not gratify the cravings and desires of the flesh (of human nature without God).*

### I Peter 5:6-7 (NIV)

*Humble yourselves, therefore, under God's mighty hand, that he may lift you up in due time. Cast all your anxiety on him because he cares for you.*

**Civil War Within**
Wind, water and fire
Bring both blessing
And curse.
Together require
Together conspire
We taste their best and
Worst.

So like siblings
Our smiles and tears
And selfish egos walk
Grow or diminish
Over the years
Continually talk.

Fear and hope
Sit hand-in-hand
I pray that I may
Understand
My joy in life …
Not made by fate
But in the choices
That I make.

It's Christ in me
That matters most
*Jesus loves me*
My only boast
My only boast.

*Mainsail Lake, Naples, Florida*

## 7

# Old Freedom

In our youth we are much like a bird on the ground, easily intimidated. As we grow older, we hopefully become less confined to the mere lateral, selfish view, more easily adopting attitudes which *build up* and avoid those that *destroy*.

Aging is part of God's redemptive plan. Contrary to the often-stereotyped generalization that the elderly become out-of-touch and less relevant, the opposite is often true. God gives us the wings of aging so that we can rise above the selfish bent of the world. Maturity is intended to deepen understanding and our capacity to forgive; it allows one to grow in peace. It's not the passive kind of harmony that blindly claims *whatever is,* is okay. Rather it's a powerful, quiet calm which comes from seeing life more fully from a comprehensive, truth-filled perspective.

Grey-haired liberty does not imply that I've earned the right to be a grump, making up more of my own rules. Rather, it is the realization that my thirst for purpose is bringing me ever closer to my Father, where my entire being flourishes! I can choose to live beyond intimidation. Now, more certainly I know my Creator God guides my footsteps and loves me. Jesus said so. Joy continues to fill my soul, new and fresh every morning.

### Psalm 46:10 (NIV)
*"Be still, and know that I am God; I will be exalted among the nations, I will be exalted in the earth."*

### Time Out
Precious Father, thank You for lifting us above the mediocrity of self; You encourage me to see Your Hand in everyday places. Jesus, Your Spirit, the Comforter, ever-moves me closer to what matters most. Amen.

### Psalms 32:8 (NIV)
*I will instruct you and teach you in the way you should go; I will counsel you with my loving eye on you.*

### Today in-Christ
I will pursue the discipline of listening intently for the Spirit's voice. May the resultant peace become both my inspiration and destination in all the seasons and chapters of my life.

**Old Freedom**
The liberty of aging
Walks with me
Joy so subtle yet bold
I'll not despair
I will not grieve
In growing old.

Too many days wasted
Pursuing *my* dreams
Apart from the Spirit's
Eye-counsel it seems.

In my Creator unfettered
My freedom is found
In the Father's good pleasure
My joy abounds.

*Little Blue Heron at Kayak Launch site, Shell Island Road, Rookery Bay, Florida*

## 8

# *Hold Fast*

The Little Blue [heron] flew in just as I was about to slip the kayak into the brackish, coastal waters. I thought it a welcoming gift and was thrilled to see this exquisite, blue wonder up close. My anticipation peaked – I was embarking on an inspiring venture! The mystery of the narrow mangrove channels was calling – fascinating, slender waterways which hold many beautiful surprises. With little effort, I would merge into the dense canopy and take a front-row seat viewing a spectacular, outdoor, 3-D cinema in living color. I crossed a couple miles of turquoise-blue, open water before heading into the dense cover of mangroves. A long narrow island captivated my interest. I found a concealed passageway into a pristine, 10-acre pond, a perfect circle. Exploring the outer perimeter, I discovered yet another, much narrower channel. I quietly followed it for perhaps a mile, vines often touching the kayak on both sides. It then opened up into a wider passage with several choices of waterways. I made another mental *map-note* of the route – and was hopeful I could find my way out again.

There was no encounter of which I didn't approve. I enjoyed numerous close-up sightings: an Osprey eating a muskrat, many varieties of herons and egrets, mullet jumping so often and so near that I thought one may soon join me in the kayak. I knew the return route would be very difficult at best. My logic contributed very little to my confidence in finding my way back to the landing. It was God's grace on my behalf that carried the day. And a beautiful day it was – being lost in a paradise of blue and exquisite wonder. Time flies when you're having fun.

Faith is a life-giving path which enables one to hope confidently, forgive quickly, laugh hilariously, care deeply – and simply persevere when we find ourselves lost near the edge.

**John 15:5 (NIV)**
*"I am the vine; you are the branches. If you remain in me and I in you, you will bear much fruit; apart from me you can do nothing."*

I have often asked God for greater faith. I praise Him, for He is always willing to give more. Most often, faith and joy come bundled together in an exuberant *fountain of realization*. These *fountains* speak to me, not in single sentences, but in entire chapters. A new aspect of God's character becomes vividly clear!

**Psalms 87:7 (NIV)**
*As they make music they will sing, "All my fountains are in you."*

Impactful and humbling, spontaneous revelations are manifested in both the simple and extraordinary. One common strand they share – they all have the same *playwright* who nurtures peace, joy and goodness. It is the passionate habit of the Holy Spirit to beautifully and carefully giftwrap His intimate messages, sending them directly to my soul. I become connected to the eternal. And I love Him all the more.

**Time Out**
Beautiful Savior, thank You for the gift of faith. I praise You for the many ways in which Your Holy Spirit handcrafts Your nurturing care and affection for me. Amen.

**Today in-Christ**
Today I'll purposefully go to a hideaway place and meditate upon what it means to be connected to the True Vine. I'll listen for the voice of the Holy Spirit and ask God for greater faith.

**Hold Fast**
I will sing of the fountains of Zion
Give praise for the Living Water
Thank Christ for the cleft in the Rock
Hold fast the Hand of my Father.

*Road to Dunklin Memorial Camp, Okeechobee, Florida*

## 9

# Healing the Past

Occasionally I meet a person whose manner and words dramatically soften and sweeten the atmosphere. Their capacity for understanding and caring makes it obvious that they have spent much quality time with Jesus. I admire such people for their *faith-walk*; I give my praise to the Holy Spirit integrated into their hearts. In the winter of 2013, I visited Dunklin, a faith-based, drug rehabilitation camp, and in that brief visit, my life was enriched enormously.

A worshipful peace settled within me that early morning as I drove east from Naples into a glorious sunrise. I became a participant in the grand *coming alive* of a new day. Palm and pine spires and lonely hammocks were peacefully silhouetted in the radiance of the red-orange-yellow glow of daybreak. The dawning light sang out praises filled with joy – a foretelling of the inspiration I would more fully realize, as the Morning Star rose even higher in my heart later that day. The final approach to Dunklin took me down a narrow, beautiful, canopied highway.

Lush, arching trees interlaced with vines symbolized a sacred, protected path. I felt I was coming to a place of faith – encouragement and healing for those in need of the Spirit's touch, and that included me.

Pastor Terrell was standing outside the fellowship hall to greet me when I arrived. He had waited for me before beginning the annual networking meeting. There were rehab counselors and staff from around the state, enjoying coffee and conversation. Pastor Terrell seemed immediately familiar to me, although I had never met him before. He stepped to the mic and softly, but confidently, began by inviting all of us to pray with him. He first asked, *"Will you put your hand over your heart as we invite God to take His rightful place within us?"*

Next, Grandma Mary, an 82-year-old woman in a wheelchair sang *Amazing Grace*. She sang so beautifully and with such passion that one would think she was the writer of that cherished old hymn. The words brought the warmth of Christ's face into the room. Clearly, the Spirit gained full command of the floor. I knew beyond a doubt that God's message would be highly impactful. Pastor Terrell then related his life-story. His personal journey to faith and healing at the hand of Jesus. The precious truth reinforced in me through Terrell's story was simply this: *The greatest joy in life is found in knowing and serving Jesus!*

Terrell's responsibilities were difficult and demanding, counseling and ministering to the 110 men who came to Dunklin for a 10-month stay. These men bring with them the waywardness of their addictions and the darkness of their past. Into their brokenness, the Dunklin team pours out the love, nurture and power of Jesus – our Almighty Public Defender. These broken men and their families begin a journey of transformation. Despair and anger are touched with Christ's mercy and hope; new skills and attitudes push aside old fears and habits.

## Time Out

Precious Father, thank You for responding to those times in my life when I need to have my faith restored and strengthened. You indeed are the most powerful change-agent of life. I praise You for Your loving-kindness, which moves our lives in tangible but mysterious ways, and never misses the mark. Amen.

## Today in-Christ

This week I'll prayerfully take inventory of my *faith-walk* and consider those behaviors and areas of my life which need to be avoided, confronted or improved. God-willing, and with His inspiration, I will act accordingly.

## *Philippians 3:8 (AMP)*

*Yes, furthermore, I count everything as loss compared to the possession of the priceless privilege (the overwhelming preciousness, the surpassing worth, and supreme advantage) of knowing Christ Jesus my Lord and of progressively becoming more deeply and intimately acquainted with Him [of perceiving and recognizing and understanding Him more fully and clearly]. For His sake I have lost everything and consider it all to be mere rubbish (refuse, dregs), in order that I may win (gain) Christ (the Anointed One).*

**Healing the Past**
Free from the penalty of my sin
Free from wayward power within
Pride defeated - a blessed loss
I bring my faults to the precious cross
Jesus, Defender of all mankind
Morning Star bringing
Light to the blind.

*Mary and Martha outside their home at Dunklin Memorial Camp, a faith-based, addiction-recovery ministry, Okeechobee, Florida, 2013*

## 10

# Sweet Spirit in This Place

The old hymns flowed out of her with powerful, fragrant conviction. She was known by the residents as *"Grandma Mary,"* and she was deeply loved. This 82-year-old woman opened the session by singing *Amazing Grace* and *I Shall Not be Moved*, a logical duo. I closed my eyes, desiring to receive the fullness of the blessing, and sensed I was looking into the face of Jesus; I felt the comfort of His presence. After the rehab-networking meeting at Dunklin, I visited with Mary in her cottage home on the Dunklin campus. I gained a profound appreciation for her life.

She began: "*I was born the first time in Savannah, Georgia, in 1930 to Kell and Lucy Hood. I was born the second time in 1946 when I made Jesus the Lord of my life.*" Mary and her husband Wilbur served as parents to thirty-one foster children over the years, and at one time they had eleven in their home. "*It was not a shelter home for the state. My husband only made $250 a week – I tell you God is very good at multiplication ... we never had a day that our needs were not met. We cared for each child for as long as they needed us. If I was not connected to Jesus the Vine, I could do nothing.*"

"*My husband retired from his work just as three of the last five children had graduated and left home. This left us free to move here to Dunklin in 1988 and join in ministering to alcohol- and drug-addicted men. My husband passed away March 24, 1998. God has allowed me and Martha, my daughter to live and work here. We sort donated clothes and other items and give to the men and their families – what they can use. Whatever is left is sold on yard sales and the money is used for other camp supplies. The most important part is that we are able to sing with the men in the evenings and give them a home atmosphere where they feel godly, family love. We pray together and share sodas and cookies; they are a blessing to us as well.*"

Grandma Mary's life inspires me to take a firmer grasp upon a vital truth: *when we fix our eyes on Jesus, He will accomplish the extraordinary within our everyday lives.* The Father's character remains the same, but His specific methods are ever-changing.

### Hebrews 12:1-2 (NIV)
*Therefore, since we are surrounded by such a great cloud of witnesses, let us throw off everything that hinders and the sin that so easily entangles. And let us run with perseverance the race marked out for us, fixing our eyes on Jesus, the pioneer and architect of faith.*

*For the joy set before him he endured the cross, scorning its shame, and sat down at the right hand of the throne of God.*

Bernard, the groundskeeper was the last person I met at Dunklin. I noticed him intently working on a small 2-acre oasis called Prayer Island. I was drawn to him, feeling there may be a blessing or insight waiting to blossom, if I just took the initiative to open the door. This is often the way the Holy Spirit makes His investments into our inner being. I walked over to say hello to this kind-faced gentleman. In a moment, he was no longer a stranger. I learned of Bernard's love for Jesus immediately. He told of how he'd made his peace with God. Most impressive was the intimacy of that relationship. *"When I go up on the ladder to trim trees,"* Bernard said, *"I say – ok now Jesus, you know I'm up here, so please send an angel to protect me."*

### Romans 8:38-39 (NIV)
*For I am convinced that neither death nor life, neither angels nor demons, neither the present nor the future, nor any powers, neither height nor depth, nor anything else in all creation, will be able to separate us from the love of God that is in Christ Jesus our Lord.*

Bernard lives in a continuing conversation with Christ throughout the day. They are inseparable – and Bernard knows it. He also spoke of the pain in his life, but continues to pray for healing for himself and others. Bernard's joy, peace and gentleness in the midst of his imperfect circumstances, are a praiseworthy reference point; a testimony to God's lavish provision and sweet care for those who know and love and trust in Him.

### Time Out
Precious Father, Your Spirit is manifested in a myriad of beautiful ways. I thank you for the lives of Grandma Mary and Bernard. I thank You for their many spiritual gifts. Lord, Your *grace* is truly

*amazing.* By faith, may my eyes be fixed on You, my ears tuned to Your voice, and may my heart be eager to obey. Amen.

## Psalm 73:25-26 (NIV)

*Whom have I in heaven but you? And earth has nothing I desire besides you. My flesh and my heart may fail, but God is the strength of my heart and my portion forever.*

## Today in-Christ

Today I'll walk in the awareness that only *in-Christ* can I live a life pleasing to Him. By His grace, *I shall not be moved,* refusing selfish compromises of honesty and character. I'll practice intentional listening.

## Isaiah 30:21 (AMP)

*Your ears will hear a word behind you, "This is the way, walk in it," whenever you turn to the right or to the left.*

## Sweet Spirit in This Place

Ordinary people, eyes fixed on Christ
Become the hands of Jesus
In our everyday lives.

Living in loss, defeat and fear
We forfeit the good He died to win
I'd rather choose to trust in Christ
Resist the lies of pride-filled sin.

When all I had was selfish me
Then ego reigned and ruled
*In-Christ* makes all the difference now
In-Him, *I'll not be moved.*

Born again, His joy we gain
Praise God, we have a choice
Undefeated by the noise
Of empty lies and selfish ways ...
Praise God – I choose
Amazing Grace.

*Nellie Jean Park, Kanabec County, Minnesota*

## 11

# *Learning to Listen*

I hadn't seen the young missionary family for several years. They came to the family farm with their six children. These youngsters found enormous fulfillment in simple enjoyments. Television, video games, and multiple cell phones are not part of their family culture. They were contented, even excited to fish in our river, comb the hair of our two miniature horses, play with the dogs, gather the eggs, run the trails and try out all the swings in our neighborhood park. It was a refreshing time of unpretentious fun. Of course, when joined by eight of my own grandchildren, everyone had an even bigger hoot. I contemplated the futures of this little community of newfound friends. It was easy to love them and want God's best for each and every one.

In sharp contrast to this picture, I had reason a few days later to interview two law enforcement staff regarding underage alcohol abuse and binge drinking. Deficiencies in parental attitudes and skills were noted by both as the key reason for the enormous problem. Children need mentors in their lives to encourage, discipline and guide them in simple, common sense.

A grandparent is in the perfect position to teach the grandchild how to listen for the Spirit's voice. I can only imagine the gains a child may make with that sort of insight!

If parents don't provide the needed encouragement, it causes a tragic and costly gap. The disparity may still be partially filled by someone who cares and is willing to make time for that child or youth. The key is time -- taking time to listen, taking time to find something positive, and then building on it. The Holy Spirit stands ready to multiply the benefits of our efforts. It's not really that difficult and the blessing flows in all directions!

Returning home from the jail staff interviews, I noticed an Amish boy with his father, walking hand-in-hand down a sidewalk in town. The boy may have been seven or eight years old. It was obvious that he was enjoying tremendously his privileged *one-on-one* time with dad. Since there are not numerous places for the Amish to park their horse-drawn buggies, these folks walk together for longer distances than most of us. *Perhaps we should consider hanging up the car keys once in a while and see what we're missing.*

Teaching parenting skills to young parents is another mentoring option. Many new parents have only marginal experience and may deeply appreciate practical instruction. The value of simple friendship is remarkably significant.

It's important not to be overwhelmed by the scope of the whole problem. Focus on one individual, perhaps beginning with one hour a week. Time invested into mentorship yields profound rewards. The TV will get along just fine without so much of our attention. Love goes a long way; it travels at *light* speed.

## Time Out
Precious Father, help our communities return to Your simple answers for our complex problems. Move in our hearts to remove excuses for not reaching out to our neighborhood when the heartbreak is so obvious. Equip us with the discernment of Your Spirit, that we may be able to seize an opportunity to demonstrate Your love to someone nearby.

## Today in-Christ
I'll ask God to show me a mentorship opportunity close to home and I'll seek His guidance as I pursue it.

## *Matthew 19:13-15 (PHILLIPS)*
*Then some little children were brought to him, so that he could put his hands on them and pray for them. The disciples frowned on the parents' action but Jesus said, "You must let little children come to me, and you must never stop them. The kingdom of Heaven belongs to little children like these!" Then he laid his hands on them and went on his way.*

**Learning to Listen**
*Dedicated to my grandchildren*

Precious youth
Please stop and listen
While you are still young.
Learn to hear the
Spirit's call
A promise whispered
A voice so small ...
Speaking love into your hearts.

Don't hesitate in fear
To look into His face
Or
Walk by too fast
When He is near ...
Embrace
And ask
For what you want
And what you need.

You and He will sort it out ...
You'll see.

*Faith-based, equine-assisted therapy, Changing Gaits rehab facility, Brook Park, Minnesota*

## 12

## Fears Defeated

Often the best recovery therapy is simply a deep and honest look at oneself. When we face our addictions, biases, selfish attitudes and destructive behaviors in a loving environment of hope, truth and transparency, amazing personal transformation can be the outcome.

I observed a training event at Changing Gaits: men and women had come to learn how to use equine-assisted therapy. While the trainers deserve much credit, there was also an inescapable presence of a loving reality – a powerful, creative and dynamic force. No doubt, that was in part the result of Guy Kaufman's passionate prayers for the event. Guy is the Founder, and his mission is *healing and horses, and the love of Jesus.* The Holy Spirit's presence covers every corner of the Ranch.

The equine exercises generally take the form of a task to be completed involving one or more horses, and usually a series of obstacles or tools, i.e., barrels, poles, orange construction cones, and hay or feed. The people in the exercise are therapy clients who often come in desperation – driven by the pain of abuse, addiction, an eroding marriage or a dysfunctional family. A few come simply for the purpose of building team-cohesiveness.

To most, a horse is an intimidating animal, easily gaining the attention and respect of the client. The therapist assigns a representative identity to the horse which may be a mission, an issue, an addictive behavior, a position in a company, a member of the family or perhaps even the life of the client. The roles, rules and the tasks of the exercise are chosen by the equine therapist. The participants attempt to complete the given tasks, and in so doing, gain significant insight into their own limitations, biases, attitudes, character strengths and weaknesses (and those of each other). The observers of the exercise are mutual beneficiaries of the therapy. The dominant key to its success, however, is the loving touch of the Master Counselor, the Holy Spirit.

### Philippians 1: 3-6 (NIV)
*I thank my God every time I remember you. In all my prayers for all of you, I always pray with joy because of your partnership in the gospel from the first day until now, being confident of this, that he who began a good work in you will carry it on to completion until the day of Christ Jesus.*

Burdens can be lifted and habits can be broken, all in the blink of an eye. But changing daily patterns of thought, attitude and behavior generally takes time – like changing the gait, the walking pattern of a horse. A seed planted in good soil requires time to germinate and grow. Maturity is not an event; it is a process, a journey. Thankfully the same Holy Spirit who opens our eyes to the truth of our situation is the same Spirit who desires to walk with us – all the way home.

## Time Out

Precious Father, thank You for the many ways You clear away the killing murkiness of my discouragements. You help me accept and learn from the consequences of my sin. Wiping away my confusion and pride, you build a new floor over my brokenness – allowing all that was wrong to be the foundation for all that is right. In Christ, I need not deny my past. I need only to build upon sincere repentance. This I do at your invitation and by your power and grace. Amen.

## Today in-Christ

I will ask God to speak to me in a series of spiritual object lessons. I'll watch carefully for his character to shine into the simple and ordinary events of my day.

## 2 Timothy 1:7 (NIV)

*For the Spirit God gave us does not make us timid, but gives us power, love and self-discipline.*

**Fears Defeated**
My weakness slain
By marvelous grace
My selfishness cast aside
In Christ I trust
On Him I lean
Each new day confide.

My fears defeated
The Spirit reigns
Today I'm lifted up
Discouragement will have no voice
I'll live in what I've gained.

*Low Lake, Ely, Minnesota*

# 13

## Family Time

Their small, eager feet hit the ground with an intense desire to run and explore this new beautiful world of lakes, bays, streams, trails and high rock walls. And so they did, for four magical days. Seven boys, ages 3-10 had waited patiently to go with grandpa to what we all generally call the Boundary Waters, less than an hour's bumpy ride north of Ely, Minnesota. Now the time had come to step into this new universe, where discovery and mystery challenge every molecule of a boy's imagination and capacity for fun. For me, it was a dream and hope *come true*; one of my life's richest blessings. Wilderness camping again with my two oldest daughters and their families was finally possible. Perhaps it was me who had most-patiently waited for this day.

On the way up, we had reviewed safety rules at Gordy's High Hat, while eating burgers and fries. We discussed a spiritual theme and enjoyed a leisure time-out for morning devotions. In the purity of this natural environment, children are extremely open and sensitive to the voice of the Comforter, the Holy Spirit. Amidst scented pines, loons and turtles, much can be achieved in the heart of a child – lessons learned that will benefit them and their friends for a lifetime.

The small, single-seat kayaks were a big hit. Two small boys easily fit into each, and off they'd go, a foursome into the bay, masters of their new domain. Lifejackets and a growing confidence served the boys well. Upon their return to camp, they told stories of nesting loons, jumping fish and high-rock ledges; bringing with them bountiful treasures of soft-edge driftwood, shiny-crayfish claws and colorful, smooth stones.

A three-mile canoe and kayak-trek to Bass Lake waterfalls, a hike to Look-Out Point, a six-pound Bass caught by Levi on a worm from Grandpa's farm, and all the fresh fish we could eat, told much of our enchanting stay.

*Prayer is Practical* became our theme. It pays to talk to God about all our life-issues, large and small. It pays to listen for His voice and seek Him first each new morning. He is powerful and He loves us big time. A simple truth, when received with child-like faith.

Around the morning and evening campfires the boys shared their object lessons and single-sentence, popcorn prayers. Treyton, age 6, said, *"Two butterflies came to the trail flying together ahead of me. Then one flew off into the woods, but the other one just stayed on the trail flying ahead of me. I think God was telling me that I should always try to stay on His path."* Brief insights and snatches of God's manifested love and wisdom became commonplace. *May it last a lifetime.*

On the return trip home, we enjoyed presenting a certificate to each of the boys, depicting one of their unique camp achievements. The ride from Ely to the ice cream shop in Cloquet allowed time for my daughters, Sara and Leah, to brainstorm and create these paper awards using a brown paper grocery bag, providing so much fun.

- Ten-year-old Cameron received the *Olympics Champion Award* by winning the ball throwing contest; the only event we had time for on pack-out morning. He was also recognized for his honesty and fairness.
- Nine-year-old Levi received the *Behemoth Bass Award* catching a six-pounder all on his own. His patience with Grandpa's excessive fishing advice was also noted.
- Nine-year-old Luke received the *Chief Kayak Adventurer* and *Loon Spotter Award.* Luke was in the kayak much of every day, bringing in regular reports of loon activity.
- Seven-year-old Justin received the *Master Mountain Goat Award* for climbing and descending Giant's Hill in record time. He not only ran up – but ran down as well!
- Six-year-old Treyton received the *Eager Beaver Fisherman* and *Prayer Warrior Award.* He really had the fishing bug and was usually first to pray at mealtime.
- Five-year-old Isaac received The Champion Crayfish Claw Collector Award. With dedication and sharp eyes, he had found a whole handful of those little colorful remnants among the shoreline rocks – keepsakes fit for a king!
- Three-year-old Timothy received the *Song in My Heart* Award for non-stop singing while on top of Daddy's shoulders. He really enjoyed that method of hiking.

**Time Out**
Precious Father, thank You for Your creative splendor in so many places, and for the many popcorn insights You lovingly deliver to young and old. Open wide our spiritual eyes and ears that we may be filled with the joy of knowing You. Amen.

**Today in-Christ**
This week with God's assistance, I'll slow my pace, sharpen my sight, unclutter my mind and watch for Him. I'll encourage a child to do the same.

*Hebrews 11:6 (NIV)*
*And without faith it is impossible to please God, because anyone who comes to him must believe that he exists and that he rewards those who earnestly seek him.*

**Family Time**
In that sacred place, at a time set apart
Meet with us Lord in your lecture hall
Teach us through snatches
Of your lovely heart
To ponder
Respond to your call.

*Mom Carlson*

## 14

# Keep Looking Up

Mother believed in the health benefits of cod liver oil. Her seven sons had to endure the foul, fishy taste of this old-time remedy. Mom knew it to be an affordable, preventative measure against the common cold and a host of other ailments. Convincing a 10-year-old that something *that bad* could be *that good* wasn't easy. For a season, mother's ways of caring for her family would prevail. Looking back, it's easy to thank God now for so much that I took for granted back then.

There were responsibilities on the farm which I didn't enjoy. I dreaded going into the dark granary to fetch oats for the livestock. I never told Dad why I hated that job so much. An old overcoat hung in the attic, which I could always see in my peripheral vision. In dim light, it seemed evil and alive.

Forking frozen silage down the silo shoot and feeding hay, were two fairly pleasant chores, but washing the udders of the cows so my brother Oscar could milk them was a dirty job. Sometimes I'd get swatted by a tail soaked in urine. Oscar and I made up a simple game to put some fun into the milking routine. We'd see who could toss the wash rag (squeezed into a ball) into the wash bucket the most times without missing. Generally, the enjoyable jobs outnumbered the others – until Dad said I'd have to do the milking and cleanup alone, so that Martin, Jerome and Oscar could get the hay bales into the barn before the rain.

One summer I got to drive the small Allis Chalmers tractor, hauling oats from the thrashing rig to the granary. That was the best job of all. I could barely reach the steering wheel and clutch pedal at the same time. I sensed I was part of something very good, something precious. Our neighborhood community harvested oats together: Eddy owned a thrashing machine, others brought their tractors and hay racks, and Dad brought his boys. Now the crew was at our farm with only two expectations: hard work and lots of good food. Each neighbor gave 100% of what they could give to the other and awaited their turn. *I've not seen a better testimony of God's love.*

### Matthew 7:12 (AMPC)
*So then, whatever you desire that others would do to and for you, even so do also to and for them, for this is (sums up) the Law and the Prophets.*

When Mom and Dad had more bills than money, patience ran shallow. I remember walking to the end of our driveway more than once to get away from some friction that had erupted between them. I had the rudiments of a working faith by that time and asked God to bring understanding and joy to me. I wanted to know why things were so difficult for my family; I wanted to feel happy. These are among the earliest prayers of my life that I can vividly remember. Martin was mowing clover hay near the end of our ¼-mile driveway. The air was fully perfumed with its sweetness. God chose to answer those childhood prayers immediately. I received a powerful portion of inner joy, which has remained with me – though only as a remnant at times. Still, in the lowest moments of my life, that same familiar joy faithfully returns and snatches me from despair.

### Proverbs 3:5- 6 (NIV)
*Trust in the LORD with all your heart and lean not on your own understanding; in all your ways submit to him, and he will make your paths straight.*

### Time Out
I praise You Father for my many blessings, but the greatest by far is Your presence. I can't fully understand the path my life has taken; I've often not listened carefully to Your voice. Still you consistently lift me up and bring fresh hope and insight, just as You did when I was 10. I *praise and thank You, Jesus!* Amen.

### Today in-Christ
I'll review and count my blessings – including cod liver oil, childhood responsibilities, the companionship of my brothers, my parents' love, and my mother's many prayers.

**Keep Looking Up**
Joy for this moment
Strength for the task
This is enough
My troubles will pass.

Today I will seek Him
Trust in His power
Sufficient His love
For my trials this hour.

*Lily Pad*

## 15

# Maker of Days

My kayak slid softly up onto the bog without making a noise. In hushed silence, I sat amidst the lily pads, humbled by the awe-inspiring beauty – soft, round faces and reflections, filled with the joy of the Lord. They expressed no opinion or judgment of me, content only in giving unmistakable praise to their Creator. I listened intently, then entered into the *energy of praise* which was all around me; a sacred moment, a most-powerful reality.

### Ephesians 3:16-19 NIV
*I pray that out of his glorious riches he may strengthen you with power through his Spirit in your inner being, so that Christ may dwell in your hearts through faith. And I pray that you, being rooted*

*and established in love, may have power, together with all the Lord's holy people, to grasp how wide and long and high and deep is the love of Christ, and to know this love that surpasses knowledge—that you may be filled to the measure of all the fullness of God.*

"*Have a great day!*" We hear and use the phrase frequently, as if it is a blessing of ours to give or possess at will – our will. Well, isn't the quality of *my* day a function of *my* attitude, *my* determination? In those moments and days when my desires are not in alignment with the Creator's will and plan, I accomplish nothing of lasting benefit. When God-consciousness is left behind and forgotten, self-willed presumption becomes a common disease among mankind. We regard divine power and authority as something we put into our little toolbox, a convenient *fix* when life becomes uncomfortable. Then, when the inevitable disappointment comes, we credit fate and say, "*It was meant to be.*" In our near-*self*-sightedness we blindly march down the road thinking we're leading the parade. We're not. It is only by God's grace that we even wake up in the morning.

### Jeremiah 9:23-24 (NIV)
*This is what the LORD says: "Let not the wise boast of their wisdom or the strong boast of their strength or the rich boast of their riches, but let the one who boasts boast about this: that they have the understanding to know me, that I am the LORD, who exercises kindness, justice and righteousness on earth, for in these I delight," declares the LORD.*

### Time Out
Precious Father, may I desire and learn to seek You in both the quiet and busy times and places of my life. Please teach me, Lord, the astonishing value of seeking You in the *now* of my life. I want to walk within Your will not mine. Help me to live more of my

moments in the power and sweetness of knowing and worshiping You. Amen.

### 2 Corinthians 6:2 (NIV)
*For he says, "In the time of my favor I heard you, and in the day of salvation I helped you." I tell you, now is the time of God's favor, now is the day of salvation.*

### Today in-Christ
I'll make time to be a silent observer of people in a busy place, while at the same time asking God to open my eyes to *His greater reality*, His breathtaking Truth, Grace and Presence. I will listen and discern carefully. I'll ask that in every *tomorrow*, His hand may guide me to places and times of worship and comfort for my soul.

### Maker of Days
There is a time
A secret place
Moments reserved for me
To enter in and gaze upon
The greater reality.

Life-forms
Both large and small
Even microbial
Whisper and call
Chanting their tributes
To one and all
Insisting their voices be heard

I look into the lily-face
And sing my song of praise
To Christ-Creator
Utmost lover
Maker and Keeper
Of all my days.

*Kuskokwim River near village of Kalskag, Alaska*

# 16

# *His Compassions Never Fail*

The mighty Kuskokwim ever plows toward the sea, continually changing course as if struggling to find a better route. Much like this meandering river, many of us push to move forward, yet ultimately remain in a valley of hopelessness. We seek a dramatic life-change, but instead by default, become the lonely captives of our private, desperate discouragement. Instead of entering the calm of forgiveness and reconciliation, we chase after shallow activities to mask unpleasant realities. Choosing possessions over peace, we rush to protect our pride, while rarely confessing our faults. Joy eludes us.

People often continue this vain and endless meandering search, with little growth or change beyond aging. What I sensed and saw in Kalskag were these same dilemmas and failures – the same adversarial darkness that attempts to diminish and destroy everyone, everywhere. However, in Kalskag, like many small, remote villages and rural towns, the manifestations of evil are more vividly apparent.

I was excited to be on this adventure, but there was a semi-dark undertone which I felt as I stepped off the small plane onto the dirt runway of Kalskag. My friend Joey and I wanted to be helpful participants in the 50-Year Jubilee celebration of the small Evangelical church, *Calvary Mission*, founded by my deceased uncle Martin Ausdahl and his wife Audrey. Their children – my cousins – have kept the light of Christ burning, cousin Mark now serving as pastor. He and his brother Dan remain in this small native, Yupik village. I was looking forward to our reunion, which I hoped would include fishing salmon in the clear stream waters entering the grey Kuskokwim. Perhaps there would be time as well to hike the majestic foothills which beckon and rise to the north.

Alcohol continues to ravage the native villages of Alaska, as evidenced in abuse and suicide rates, nearly three times the US national average. During my brief five-day visit, there was a reckless death due to food poisoning, facilitated by alcohol-impaired judgment. A violent rape occurred, for which two teen boys were being hunted by State troopers. Adding enormously to the tragic drama, a youth shot himself and died the next morning in the humble village clinic. He was 17 years old and had shown much promise in his apprentice ability to navigate barges on the tricky Kuskokwim. A blanket of familiar sadness crept into the small village of only 350 people.

The Jubilee kick-off event was a riverside bonfire and feed for everyone in the village. Villagers up and down river had been invited. A small crowd began to gather as Mathew, guitarist, and Kevin, vocalist (both young adults from Anchorage), began to bring a message of hope in song. *"The Rock won't move … And His word is strong … And His love can't be undone."* Many had been praying that the Holy Spirit would bring a love-filled, Christ-impact to the youth of Kalskag. We asked God for a native youth to assist us with this opening event, one that had a strong testimony for what Christ had done in their battle against alcohol and drugs. In my first two days at Kalskag, no one surfaced – until 20 minutes before we began, when a young man joined the gathering. I approached him and soon learned his life story.

Phillip was from another village on the Kuskokwim. He had just arrived to do an insulation job for his company. He willingly shared with the youth his story, how his sister Minnie was his closest and best friend – until recently. She died suddenly from alcohol poisoning one very cold night after passing out. Phillip was heartbroken. He told of how he saw a Gideon Bible in the waiting room and opened it. He said, *"Romans 6 caught my eye and convicted me. I was abusing God's grace and using God's love as a license to sin. Repeatedly, after a night of drinking and drugging, I thought I could just ask God to forgive me in the morning and I'd be free to do it all over again. Then, I realized that Jesus was calling me out of a life of drugs to follow Him."* He praises God for allowing great good to come from terrible loss.

Phillip was fully prepared and joyfully willing to share his story with everyone that night, August 15, 2013. I believe all who listened received a profound blessing from the Holy Spirit.

### Lamentations 3:19-24 (NIV)

*I remember my affliction and my wandering, the bitterness and the gall. I well remember them, and my soul is downcast within me. Yet this I call to mind and therefore I have hope: Because of the LORD's great love we are not consumed, for his compassions never fail. They are new every morning; great is your faithfulness. I say to myself, "The LORD is my portion; therefore I will wait for him."*

### Time Out

Precious, caring Father, in Christ's name we come against the evil of alcoholism and drug addiction in the villages, towns and cities of America. Holy Spirit rescue these youth who so often fall into despair and violence as they are ravaged by addictions. May Your joy and love become real to them through the demonstrated compassion of Jesus Christ. Amen.

### Today in-Christ

This week I'll write a note of encouragement to someone who is shining forth the light of Christ in a dark place.

### His Compassions Never Fail

Native youth on Kuskokwim
Dance upon river, walk with wind
God-given heritage, where did it go
Vanished so quickly, nobody knows.

Lost in the darkness, children still gaze
Look in their eyes, hear what they say
*Mother I need you, Father please stay*
In drunken stupor will we turn away?

Abandoned, confused, the young go on
Few choose wisely, many fall down
Become parents of hopelessness
In alcohol drown.

New generation, a meandering stream
With heavy hearts follow that which has been
Crying and dying the young call out
*I've seen enough*, they angrily shout.

Who has the answer, where is the Light
Can no one stop this perpetual blight?

Who – but the faithful One: God-man.
Only in Christ are we able to stand.

*50-Year Jubilee Reunion, Calvary Mission Church, Kalskag Cemetery, Alaska*

## 17

# Lord, Lift Up Our Eyes

The remote Kalskag cemetery overlooks the mighty Kuskokwim River. From its quiet hillside perch, the graveyard keeps watch as the powerful river continues its meandering, forceful search for a better path to the sea. I stood with our small group from Calvary Mission Church as we pondered what may have been the wisdom, regrets and heartaches of those hushed lives. It was a lonely place of weather-beaten crosses and gravestones; a silent place where one could almost hear the whispers of bygone days. One of our group, Matthew age 23, was inspired to pray an ambitious, unusual prayer, asking the Holy Spirit to touch the hearts of all the surviving relatives, with His life-changing presence and grace. I asked the group if they believed God would hear such a prayer.

Solomon, age 24, immediately said "God hears all our prayers." I felt the Father smiling. It was a sweet, supernatural moment which I'll always cherish. My plans for a group hike up the mountain had been dampened by rain. Still, it seemed we were off to a good start.

Aviva, age 11, prayed that God would continue to walk with us around the village. We moved on to the tiny clinic where a youth age 17, was dying from a self-inflicted gunshot. He passed later that morning. We felt the heartbreak of the young man's family as people with grieving faces would come and go. Martin age 11, the youngest in our assembly, didn't understand the whole story but prayed. *"God, please heal whoever is sick."* After a few minutes we moved on. I felt God was pleased with young Martin's prayer.

Healing takes many forms.

Next, we stopped near an old, rust-orange truck discarded and hidden in the bushes. I realized then, that what was to be a hike into the hills, had become a prayer-walk with a specific spiritual purpose. So typical – the Holy Spirit took my plan and transformed it into so much more. (See Isaiah 55). The old, rusted truck became a symbol of all the *stuff in our lives* that will soon pass away.
I asked, *"Why is so much of our energy spent accumulating and caring for stuff that will not last?* It distracts us from that which is so much more important: our relationships. Both require care and feeding. We all understood and agreed. *It is far more satisfying to invest in people.* Young Martin suggested that it would be a good idea to ask God *"to take away our love of stuff,"* and so again, we prayed. The light rain continued, and we would soon be drenched, but no one minded. The shower softened our hearts and increased the intimacy of our diverse crew.

*2 Kings 6:17 (NIV)*
*And Elisha prayed, and said, Lord, I pray thee, open his eyes, that he may see. And the Lord opened the eyes of the young man; and he saw: and, behold, the mountain was full of horses and chariots of fire round about Elisha.*

We were getting cold. Emerging from the village on the north road, we looked up into the beautiful foothills. God had shown us truths that would endure for a lifetime. It was time to get back to shelter. As a conclusion to our God-arranged prayer walk, I read Psalms 91:14-16. The passage spoke to us saying, *It pays to be careful where we place our devotion and affections.* We had been abundantly fed from the hand of the Holy Spirit. I felt the joy of heaven. Praise God!

*Psalm 91:14-16. (NIV).*
*"Because he loves me," says the Lord, "I will rescue him; I will protect him, for he acknowledges my name. He will call on me, and I will answer him; I will be with him in trouble, I will deliver him and honor him. With long life I will satisfy him and show him my salvation."*

**Time Out**
Precious Lord, help me to never underestimate the enormity of Your love or the reach of Your hand. I ask for greater love and greater faith. Amen.

**Today in-Christ**
I'll walk around my neighborhood and ask God to touch the lives and hearts of those I know and of those who are complete strangers. I will ask the Father to drive out the fear and reluctance which surround this inspiration.

**Lord, Lift Up Our Eyes**
Though I'm filled with fear and doubt
I'll wait for you Lord … at the Spirit's call
For when I'm feeling very small
You lift my gaze unto the hills
And the Heavenly Host stands tall.

*View from the high ridge above Kalskag, Alaska*

## 18

# No Room for Doubt

My new friend Phillip asked if I'd like to ride up into the high foothills overlooking the Kuskokwim. Yes, of course, so I climbed on his 4 wheeler, leaving at about 8:30 p.m. He sped along the rough trail higher and higher. At times I felt I needed to lean as far forward as possible to keep from tipping over backward. I asked him to slow down a bit for the sake of my 65-year-old back. He was so eager to show me the splendor of the high ridge above the village. I was thrilled, having just seen the dynamic power of the Holy Spirit. Two hours earlier Phillip had been the amazing answer to my prayers for a strong, youth-witness regarding the perils of alcohol, drug abuse, and the grace of Christ. My doubts were defeated; my prayers lavishly answered. Phillip spoke so eloquently and tenderly to the youth and young adults gathered on the shore of the Kuskokwim for the Calvary Mission Jubilee bon-fire. We both knew God's sovereign hand had managed the events of that evening. True to character, Christ's light shown into the darkness of the village. As we climbed higher and higher, I wondered, *"What surprise does God have in store for us now?*

I have often been privileged to experience extreme joy and beauty in both obscure and extraordinary events, places and times. Am I giving myself a commendation? I hope not. To step into pure joy is to experience a personal gift from the *Father of Lights* – a gift which one should never take for granted. Joy and beauty, these two qualities most often travel together. Such was the case when Phillip and I arrived atop the high ridge above Kalskag, a place he laughingly named, "Heaven."

It was now 10:00 p.m. The valley to the left of the ridge was filled with the lovely, vibrant light of the setting sun in the west. I gazed carefully into the bottom land, fully expecting to see a moose or bear emerge for night feeding. Shadows were filling in and steadily moving across the valley to the east. Phillip whispered to me, *"Isn't it beautiful – praise God!"* This phrase became the theme of the evening. I knew with utter confidence that God was blessing us with His gift of affirmation. Unspeakable elation nearly took my breath away. My newly discovered brother Phillip felt it too. At times like this, when I vividly sense the presence and power of the Holy Spirit, I grow tremendously in my faith. I comprehend more fully the grandeur and capacity of my loving Savior. I become more intimately acquainted with my own limitations; I am humbled to the core. There is no place left for pride. *The praise service earlier in the evening had been blessed; Phillip's testimony was still resonating within me and others too – I was sure.* Now God was crowning His victory here, high above the village, allowing us to commune with Him, as we became engrafted into the spectacular hush of this stillness and splendor. Few words were spoken; they were unnecessary.

When we turned to look back to the south, we saw something very strange! There standing on a knoll we'd just passed was a large, wild animal about 1/4 mile away. We looked intently, but could not determine what it was. It had the size of a mature grizzly and looked bulky about the front shoulders, but neither of us was convinced it was a bear. It certainly wasn't a moose. For nearly five minutes, we quietly pondered the sight, as the animal continued its slow amble across the top and then over the edge and out of sight. That was our opportunity to approach much closer. We gained considerable ground and at our next sighting were able to determine what it was. Unbelievably – it was a large, mature Musk Ox, probably a lone bull. He turned to face us directly, as if to say, *"Come closer if you dare."* His horns were massive; he showed no fear of us. As the wind changed a bit, we could faintly smell him. This was indeed a rare prospect as the Musk Ox is very rare in this area of Alaska. Most of the native people of Kalskag have never seen one! I praise God to be among the few to have seen this ruggedly handsome creature in the Alaskan wild. Some may choose to dismiss the whole experience as adventuresome luck. I choose to call it an intimate blessing from my heavenly Father, a treasured moment which I'll always cherish.

The sun fell asleep in the west and darkness was slipping in with a raw, damp chill in the air. We headed back down the ridge with smiles deep inside. I had gained a clearer concept of *the eternal* and of that which is *holy.*

**Time Out**
Creator God, You own the cattle on a thousand hills. Thank You for the exquisite surprises You drop into my path; they ever-remind me of who really matters. You brought Phillip into my

life at a critical time and provided his testimony for the benefit of many. Then You chose to put frosting on the top of that already delicious day; you guided us to *heaven*. I thank and praise you! Amen.

**Today in-Christ**
Do I want to grow in my faith? If the answer is "yes," then I'll ask God to work circumstantially in my life this week to allow and encourage me to trust Him more.

*John 1:1-5 (NIV)*
*In the beginning was the Word, and the Word was with God, and the Word was God. He was with God in the beginning. Through him all things were made; without him nothing was made that has been made. In him was life, and that life was the light of all mankind. The light shines in the darkness, and the darkness has not overcome it.*

**No Room for Doubt**
Crushing my doubt
You come to my aid
Rescue complete and secure
Redeemed from my pride
And all my mistakes
You love me
Of this I am sure.

*Mississippi River*

## 19

# Watch Care

Do you have a guardian angel? Although I rarely think about it, I answer, *"Yes."* My opinion stems from two back-to-back events which occurred years ago. I was hunting grouse along the Mississippi River with Buster, the best hunting dog I'd ever owned. We had hunted in this area before with my brothers and I knew it well. As I walked along the river's edge in the perfect cover for grouse, one flushed and flew directly across the river. Cold, white frost was everywhere, and a fresh snow had fallen that morning. It was one of those enchanted winter mornings when both Jack Frost and snowflakes clung to everything above ground.

I hurriedly crossed the river and we searched up-river along the brush-covered bank for about 100 yards. The bird had given us the slip as they often do. I crossed the river again and returned downstream to my first point of crossing. I was shocked. The middle of the river was open water, more than 20 yards wide and 100 yards long, and flowing fast. I became sick inside as I looked at the black water convulsing in the center of that white expanse. The current was fast, so the ice had been thin. The early morning was extremely cold, so ice had temporarily formed, only to be melted again under the new insulating snow cover. I crossed in that very place no more than 30 minutes earlier! How had I not considered the possibility of thin ice? I felt foolish, humbled – and earnestly thankful. I knew full well I may not have survived, had I broken through out there in the deep middle. The Mississippi is a killing-river to which many families can attest. For an instant I was vividly aware that this could have been my end. I didn't know that a second, more serious encounter was literally waiting around the corner.

Buster and I continued our walk along the river working the alder-brush, hoping to flush another grouse. The dark stretches of open water in the middle of the river were a constant reminder of the close call I had just barely escaped. I resolved to never again be so foolish as to venture onto river ice without knowing its thickness. (It was a resolution I would necessarily break within the hour.) The river which flows through my farm is generally so shallow that one would have to search for a place to drown – but not so here.

Grouse hunting quickly pulled my concentration back and those dark thoughts vanished, but only for minutes. Buster was a dog for which I was apparently willing to risk my life. Of course, I didn't know that beforehand. When the moment came, there was no plan but only an instinctive reaction. I do not remember the event with even the least bit of heroic accomplishment – only thankfulness. A lone Mallard duck, a beautiful late season drake, dropped into the open wedge of water in the middle, and Buster was after him immediately. The duck had caught his eye before mine, and by the time I cleared the brush, he was approaching within a few feet of the open water. The duck lifted and flew only a short distance to the end of the open water downstream and Buster was swimming hard at it. I was within fifty yards when the drake flew off. I saw Buster struggling to leave the river's current and get up onto the ice. He was quickly moving to the end of the open water. I knew once he was swept under the ice he would never be seen again. It was not a question of *what* to do or *how* to do it – only could I do it *soon enough?* I had to get a large, nearby, dead-tree branch broken off and onto the ice – fast. I laid on top of it and scooted out to the water's edge within only a few feet of the point where the dark open water disappeared beneath the ice. Buster was terrified and sensed the danger. He had been thrashing and losing ground for nearly a minute. When I grabbed his front leg, he was only seconds away from certain death. That's when I first thought about my own skin.

Buster came out with a jerk and piled right on top of me, increasing my weight by 70 pounds more. What poor timing for a dog to passionately love his master! I inched away from the open water back to the thicker ice near the shore. We made it. Within the span of 60 minutes, that river had two chances to suck me in. As I walked back to the car, I wondered how and when I would ever have been found. I also thought about angels and grace – concepts that seldom mix with men in their prime.

**Psalm 91:11 (NIV)**
*For he will command his angels concerning you to guard you in all your ways.*

**Time Out**
This week I will find a quiet, private place and pray aloud with praise and thanks to my gracious Father who lavishes unseen grace and favor upon my life. *Thank You, Holy Spirit, for the angels you command. Thank You, Lord, for your preserving watch care over my heart, as well as my life.*

**Psalm 91:15 (NIV)**
*The word of the Lord: He will call on me, and I will answer him; I will be with him in trouble, I will deliver him and honor him.*

**Watch Care**
Angel, are you there
Walking ahead or behind
Who are you … where are you …
Help me to trust and find
Faith unwavering
In what I cannot see
Knowing I can surely trust
Beyond the finite me.

*Tree fort*

## 20

# Sanctuary

Children love hideouts. I'm sure you probably had one. I've had many and still have a few. As a kid I shared them with friends – cousins mostly. They would visit our farm and I would take them to my hideout in the woods or in the straw stack. Later I built a few with my own children and we named them. *Little Switzerland* was the most elaborate. Nestled into a deep ravine, overlooking a small, ambitious creek, it was fully equipped with an access rope, swing and draw bridge – dangerous to a fault, but offering bold fun for all.

*Birch Fort* was more of a *secret hideout* built with my son, Josh. Of course, building a hideout is always the best part of having one.

Today, my *hideouts* are comfortable sitting places, sanctuaries within a half-mile of my farm. To me, a *sanctuary* is a place where *the child in each of us* can run and hide. We can go there to process our questions, grief and discouragement, or go there simply to rest in God's beauty and forgiveness. It is both a refuge and fortress of security and assurance. The Spirit never fails to sit with me and bring His quiet understanding to my many questions.

*Psalm 63:1-3 (NIV)*
*You, God, are my God, earnestly I seek you; I thirst for you, my whole being longs for you, in a dry and parched land where there is no water. I have seen you in the sanctuary and beheld your power and your glory. Because your love is better than life, my lips will glorify you.*

**Time Out**
Thank You, precious Father for those places and times of listening and healing, where I may enter into the *calm* of Your presence. When You call me to the sanctuary, it is always for my benefit. I gain greater compassion for people, all precious in Your sight. I'm filled with gratitude for your goodness and grace, which you pour into our lives in so many quiet ways. I become more patient, even with myself. Thank You.

*Mark 6: 31b (NIV) Words of Jesus to the apostles.*
*"Come with me by yourselves to a quiet place and get some rest."*

**Today in-Christ**
I'll renew my familiarity with one of the neglected sanctuaries in my life.

**Sanctuary**
We live our lives
In noisy places
Ignore the longings
Of our soul
Tolerate misgivings
Deaf to the Savior's call.

Blinded by my problems-
Downhearted I become
Praise God
He then reminds me
To my sanctuary – run.

*Three Bar Ranch, Montana*

## 21

# Whispered Truth

Mother Nature is an exquisite actress, ever-performing in the Master's grand theater. Her messages come whispered through the whistling wings of low-flying geese. Her stories of joy and suffering are murmured in the wind, moving through tall pines. Menacing cloud-faces in anxious skies, speak warnings or simply entertain. An urgent note may be wrapped inside the gurgling creek-flow, or within the distinctive scent of clover or sage. I often-ponder the intentions of this friendly conspiracy, sometimes receiving specific inspiration or admonishments, like arrows that are hidden, but surely aimed at me. I listen but do not fully understand.

Alone in the woods, swamps, fields, foothills, mountains or prairie, I'm often moved by a captivating thought or inclination from beyond. The voice of the Holy Spirit speaks through the curtains of Christ's magnificent creation. Sometimes He asks questions; always, He provides answers and healing too. His soft words may bring sudden delight, the surprise of an uplifted attitude. I may receive a personal warning or feel His manifested sadness and sorrow convicting me for my part in humanity's selfish choices. Of this I am certain: the Spirit's voice is always beneficial.

### Psalm 32:8 (NIV)

*I will instruct you and teach you in the way you should go; I will counsel you with my loving eye on you.*

### Time Out

Awesome God, thank You for Your watch-care over me. The fruitfulness of my life depends upon Your presence and intimate communion; I desire to meet You in the secret places of the Most High. May I always be attentive to Your voice and ever-eager to receive Your healing touch. Amen.

### Psalms 91:1 (AMPC)

*He who dwells in the secret place of the Most High shall remain stable and fixed under the shadow of the Almighty [Whose power no foe can withstand].*

### Today in-Christ

I'll dress for the weather (whatever it is) and silently sit outside in some private sanctuary. I will empty myself of *self* and leave the results up to the Most High God.

**Whispered Truth**
Creek-bottom, red brush
Curves its way along
Defines the water's path
Shelters the water's song.

Approaching soft, I listen
Come close and standing still
Drink deep within the hush
Submit to the Father's will.

Water's bubbling voice
Beckons me *come in*
Gives me but one choice
*Sit down and please begin.*

Hidden in this refuge
Concealed near the stream
Confession meets encouragement
Sweet healing unforeseen.

I sat a long, lone while
Emptied the well of my soul
Forgiveness and understanding
Making me once again whole.

*Abandoned prairie homestead, northwestern Montana*

## 22

# *Legacy*

There was a friendly, yet imposing message coming from the prairie grass. I listened carefully, quietly waiting. Was it a song or a statement whispered? It came to me as a profound story with a warm presence. I couldn't discern its meaning at first. I just stood and gazed with deep respect at the old homestead many miles from any road. The passion and intensity of the men, women and children who once lived here – in this very place – was overwhelming. Their labor was everywhere obvious – their investments of skill, time and enormous energy stood distinct and deliberate. Theirs had been a life of endless hard work, and I sensed it had been a life of much joy as well. Rusted machinery, heavily worn and broken, lay scattered about. Trees had grown between wheel spokes while their branches consumed the brittle strands of rusted barbed-wire fences. Weather-beaten window frames and floor boards twisted with age, were still proudly struggling to retain their man-given form and place.

Then haunting questions came like early-morning-visitors to a graveyard. *What ultimate purpose did these pioneer lives serve? What was the nature of their legacy?* Their earnest strivings were still so evident. Yet, so soon their names and deeds are forgotten. *Did their lives end in victory or defeat?*

All my lingering questions could be answered in the last: *Was the love of God well-received and nurtured in this home?* I sensed these people had left behind a glorious heritage, having the capacity to live fulfilled, in spite of hardship. I hoped that *in-Christ* they had found their completeness, well-acquainted with the rich fruits of the Spirit. I prayed that their descendants, too, would put their trust in Him.

In this obscure place, I felt God's abiding presence and joy amidst the prairie grass.

**Ephesians 1:18 (NIV).**
*I pray that the eyes of your heart may be enlightened in order that you may know the hope to which he has called you, the riches of his glorious inheritance in his holy people.*

**Time Out**
Precious Father, *owner of the cattle on a thousand hills,* plant deep within me an awareness of the many, bountiful benefits and promises You give to those who seek to know. Lord, I praise you for *the riches of my inheritance in-Christ.* Amen.

**Today in-Christ**
I'll prayerfully consider three values (or truths) and ask the Lord
to make them the treasured cornerstone of my life and my family
legacy.

*Matthew 6:20-21 (KJV)*
*But lay up for yourselves treasures in heaven, where neither moth*
*nor rust doth corrupt, and where thieves do not break through nor*
*steal: For where your treasure is, there will your heart be also.*

**Legacy**
Faces soon forgotten
Our sweetest memories pass
Dim voices growing older
History covers over
In wind-blown, prairie grass.

What is, will not remain
Today will not sustain
Nothing to which we cling
Nothing we can give or bring
To the lives of those who follow.
Has my living been so hollow?

What of us will be remembered
One generation nigh?
Our might and knowledge, fancied things
Endure no more than dead-moth wings
Oh my, how time does fly.

Still something of surpassing worth
Calls to me at close of day
Rare and priceless words so pure
So precious; they alone endure

# RENEWAL

They alone will surely stay
When all the other voices fade

And we have marched our last parade
Yes, even then three words will stand
Championing the Hope of Man
*I Love You*
Rings the message clear
Spoken to all with receiving ear
Three words Christ speaks through all of Time
I pray I may receive as mine
Three words not only said but done
God's gift to us: His precious Son
Christ lived to die and lives again
Reaching for the heart of Man.

The measure of a life lived-well
Never found in power or wealth
But in the sacrifice God made
The treasure is in what He gave
And by His grace has proven true
God's living legacy
*I Love You.*

May we first receive from Him
Then boldly pass it on again
When all within this life has passed
*I Love You*
Sings the prairie grass.

*Devlin Ranch, Terry, Montana*

## 23

# Eternal

Soon forgotten, they are cast off and begin their elemental return to the earth. All vehicles one day stop and never run again. But not so with people! The seed of the eternal has been sown in every human soul, and it longs to grow up and go home. Some may prefer to view humanity as having only an earthly existence with a final ending called *death*. Yet, I think most people innately know or at least suspect, that this is not the case, for God has placed eternity in the heart of man.

*Ecclesiastes 3:11 NIV*
*He has made everything beautiful in its time. He has also set eternity in the human heart; yet no one can fathom what God has done from beginning to end.*

In a way, it's tempting to convince ourselves that there is no *afterlife*. Then, there would likely be no ultimate reckoning, no accountability for the willful selfishness done here and now. Trusting in Jesus Christ does bear a price: the subordination of our will to His. That is indeed a problem: our human will doesn't naturally desire to be in second place. So, I may try to fool myself by adopting a pseudo-rational excuse for unbelief and disobedience. God asks, *"How's that working out for you?"* In the short run, our selfish choices may prove practical because they appear *less demanding*, but only until the evil taskmaster of this world, Satan, comes to collect his rent. A quick look around at this world tells us there's a gross lack of enduring peace and joy in our communities. God's peace belongs to those who trust and follow Jesus Christ.

*2 Corinthians 5:1 (NIV)*
*For we know that if the earthly tent we live in is destroyed, we have a building from God, an eternal house in heaven, not built by human hands.*

**Time Out**
Creator God, thank You for allowing me to trek over the western prairies; they often spill over with surprises. The vistas in every direction bring freedom and nourishment to my soul. Truly, You are the Master playwright and *eternal* Sustainer of life. I trust in Your Plan. Amen.

*Daniel 4:34 (NIV)*
*At the end of that time, I, Nebuchadnezzar, raised my eyes toward heaven, and my sanity was restored. Then I praised the Most High;*

*I honored and glorified him who lives forever. His dominion is an eternal dominion; his kingdom endures from generation to generation.*

## Today in-Christ
I will ask the Lord Jesus Christ to help me know Him better; to become more real and precious to me.

## Romans 15:13 (NIV)
*May the God of hope fill you with all joy and peace as you trust in him, so that you may overflow with hope by the power of the Holy Spirit.*

## Eternal
I cannot comprehend
Or wrap my little mind
Around endless time
The beginning or the end
I just don't understand
But it's enough for me
To leave the science
Of eternity
To the One who made the Plan.

*Pelicans at roost*

## 24

# Coming Home

The familiar joy of coming home is a sweetness tasted by most of us at one time or another. For those blessed with the *comforts of home*, we find familiar security and rest. Yet, there coexists a longing for the mysterious, the unknown, and the miraculous. This yearning is a gift from God, an appetite for the supernatural. Some walk closer to the edge of the *unfamiliar* than others. Having been given an innate desire to gaze into the pool of eternity, some inquire about issues of destiny, the meaning of life and what lies ahead. It is this force in the well of our souls which prompts us to query beyond the obvious reality of our world.

*Jerimiah 33:3(NIV)*
*'Call to me and I will answer you and tell you great and unsearchable things you do not know.'*

Our Advocate, the Holy Spirit, prompts us to ask searching, spiritual questions. We are compelled to dig deeper for truth and meaning. It is this same voice of our Advocate/Comforter which calls us to *hope*. He provides us with the initiative and creative power required to see through and move beyond the emptiness of our selfish, prideful nature, yielding within us a passion to live a life enriched with goodness, beauty, and surprise. Continuously and faithfully, the "gift-giver" urges us forward on our journey, with the *hope* that we will come home at sunset.

*John 14: 25-26 (NIV)*
*"All this I have spoken while still with you. But the Advocate, the Holy Spirit, whom the Father will send in my name, will teach you all things and will remind you of everything I have said to you.*

There is another power operative which seeks to sabotage our homecoming. Routinely, the lure of excessiveness, perversion and addiction, summons us to become a law unto ourselves by making egocentric choices. Tragically, we often listen to these destructive expressions and willfully step with one foot into a self-serving misery. With only one eye looking toward heaven, our vision is impaired; we only see through our dark bias. The way home is obscured. Yes, God is gracious and He is also just. Repentance is both reasonable and practical. When I willfully wound the heart of the Protector/Lover of my soul, asking forgiveness and setting a new course is the only loving option available. To do otherwise is selfishness; it is to not act in love.

### John 14:23, 27 (NIV)

*Jesus replied, "Anyone who loves me will obey my teaching. My Father will love them, and we will come to them and make our home with them. [27] Peace I leave with you; my peace I give you. I do not give to you as the world gives. Do not let your hearts be troubled and do not be afraid.*

### Time Out

Precious Father, may I seek Your will each new day and be renewed *in-Christ* every morning! Help me to run toward Your gentle call upon my life. As I am drawn to the edges of my understanding, may I rest confident in Your goodness. This alone is my true peace, my security. Teach me, Lord, to regard You as my Lord and King. I praise and thank You. Amen.

### Today in-Christ

I will ask God to instill in me a true spirit of repentance, that I may live more aware and respectful of the values of Jesus Christ. I will ask for greater love, faith and wisdom which He promises to freely give.

### John 10: 9-10 (NIV)

*I am the gate; whoever enters through me will be saved. They will come in and go out, and find pasture. The thief comes only to steal and kill and destroy; I have come that they may have life, and have it to the full.*

### Coming Home

The Gate through which I entered:
Christ, the Door, the Way,
Became the Truth in Whom I live.
By grace, I trust,
By faith, I walk,
All praise to Christ I give.

*Osprey with Mullet*

## 25

# Not on My Terms

In a moment it was over; one life ended and another life nourished. The Osprey dove to the water and snatched up the Mullet, then flew with its prize to a high, nearby perch to enjoy dinner. I was privileged to witness this 4-second event, seeing up-close in detail with camera in hand, that nature has two faces – beautiful and severe. Both qualities move together as one – *indivisible*.

Even so it is with God's mercy and justice. Can we receive and benefit from God's mercy while turning our back to His righteousness? His kindness always walks beside his integrity. They are *inseparable*. And so it should be with our response: our love and obedience must also walk together. We are called to live holy, Christ-like lives. Our Heavenly Father lavishly stacked the deck in favor of living *in-Him* rather than *in-self*. How? By giving us the supreme advantages of His Son and His Spirit.

### John 14:23-24 (NIV)

*Jesus replied, "Anyone who loves me will obey my teaching. My Father will love them, and we will come to them and make our home with them. Anyone who does not love me will not obey my teaching. These words you hear are not my own; they belong to the Father who sent me.*

Still, it is our daily choice to walk towards Him or away. We do play a part in our salvation, not in terms of merit, for truly, Christ Alone has made a Way for us. Yet we have a responsibility in terms of our response – the surrendering of our will day by day.

### Philippians 2:13 (AMP)

*[Not in your own strength] for it is God Who is all the while effectually at work in you [energizing and creating in you the power and desire], both to will and to work for His good pleasure and satisfaction and delight.*

### Time Out

Precious Father, forgive me when I sugar-coat my faith and follow only the Church of Self-Convenience. Teach me to pursue the disciplines of obedience and the character-improvement principles set forth in Your Word, that I may know You and embrace both the liberty and the uprightness of Christ's grace. Amen.

### Titus 2:11 (AMP)

*For the grace of God (His unmerited favor and blessing) has come forward (appeared) for the deliverance from sin and the eternal salvation for all mankind.*

**Today in-Christ**
Realizing that to love God is to obey God, I will invite him to stir within my attitude this week greater devotion to His standards and values.

**Not on My Terms**
Our grief He'll cover
Our heartaches He'll share
But make no mistake
We too
Have a cross to bear.

*Carlson Farm*

## 26

# Hiding Place

*"I'm going to run away."*

Mother's response was, *"Okay, I'll get you a suitcase for your things."*

I was 6 or maybe 7 years old at the time; I recall feeling a bit deflated at her answer. But that injustice was overshadowed by the excitement of actually leaving the house on my own. I quickly gathered supplies into my small suitcase. Canned goods were too heavy and hard to open, so I took those neat little square containers of spices – lots of them. Out the door I marched toward the barn, wondering exactly where and how I'd build my new home, my own *secret place*. Young children are always fascinated with the thought of a hideout or tree fort – a sanctuary for fun and adventure. Behind the barn, at the edge of the known world, I decided to bore a hole into the baled straw stack. Removing four bales, my new home was complete. The spices looked neat; all stacked in the corner. My success soon became boring and empty. I returned home in about an hour. Mother was happy to see me.

Escaping our disappointments and the consequences of our selfish choices is a desire inherent in living. I know of no one who enjoys pain, embarrassment, or suffering. It seems equally characteristic of the human condition to *run away* to the wrong place. Idolatry and addiction make poor substitutes for the love of Jesus Christ. Tree forts make poor dwellings. As adults we eventually come to realize that our hideout is severely lacking and unfulfilling. We have a choice: find another hideout or go home to our true sanctuary.

**Time Out**
Precious Father, You seek me every day. Every moment You stand near the door of my soul and lovingly say, *"Welcome home! May I lift you up today?"* You alone are ever-faithful in caring for me. Thank You. I praise You.

**Today in-Christ**
This week I'll not neglect going home for my morning visit in His sanctuary, the secret place of the Most High.

**Psalms 32:7 (NIV)**
*You are my hiding place; you will protect me from trouble and surround me with songs of deliverance.*

*Hebrews 4:16 (NIV)*
*Let us then approach God's throne of grace with confidence, so that we may receive mercy and find grace to help us in our time of need.*

*Psalms 91:1 (AMP)*
*He who dwells in the secret place of the Most High shall remain stable and fixed under the shadow of the Almighty [Whose power no foe can withstand].*

**Hiding Place**
By faith I run to my secret place
Knowing that He cares
There I gaze upon His face
His peace and joy we share.

*Sunset on Beach*

## 27

# *Being Present*

*Then* and *now* are two very different realities; we live in both every day. *"Then"* includes yesterday and tomorrow. *"Now"* is that tiny, powerful wedge of time in-between. *"Now"* determines the character and flavor of *all* my days. But like two dominant, jealous, big brothers, *yesterday* and *tomorrow* steal as much of my attention from *now* as possible. Thus, it is a continuing struggle to be *present*. Our thoughts are so easily pulled back or pushed ahead. Only by living *now* can I be present enough to hear, really hear, the voices around me. Some are those voices of people I love; some are the beckoning of the Holy Spirit speaking in the wind or trees or in the waves on the shore. *Be still, listen; enter into communion with me.*

The fullness of our lives is found in what we receive and share *now* in the present. It's not a new dilemma. We all wrestle with being *present*, consciously and unconsciously. Too often, the needs of others are lost in the competition for my attention. Deep in my soul, I remain convicted. Jesus Christ desires to be the Lord of my heart.

### Psalms 32:8-9 (NIV)

*I will instruct you and teach you in the way you should go; I will counsel you with my loving eye on you Do not be like the horse or the mule, which have no understanding but must be controlled by bit and bridle or they will not come to you.*

Being present is about listening intently and comprehending the essence of the moment. Past regrets and future concerns are commonplace; they pull us away and shadow over the kernel of the moment. But what appears important often fades in the full spectrum of eternity. The following question may serve to make my point. Which would you desire to have as the epitaph on your tombstone?

*He was busy and accomplished much.*
or ...
*He listened, he loved, he understood.*

Activity is neither a blessing nor a curse. I appreciate those industrious people who know how to get things done. But to be habitually absent in spirit is selfishness. When my routine leaves little room to hear and empathize with others, then I know without a doubt, that I've lost control of a critically vital balance in my life. By God's grace, I must find a way to clean the garage and still welcome my grandchild's next question.

**Time Out**
Father God, when the demands of my day exceed my ability to practice a healthy balance between *doing* and *being*, I ask You to step into my path and change my course. I invite Your help in ordering my priorities. Amen.

*2 Corinthians 6:2 (NIV)*
*For he says, "In the time of my favor I heard you, and in the day of salvation I helped you." I tell you, now is the time of God's favor, now is the day of salvation.*

**Today in-Christ**
I will carefully review the activities in the week ahead and prayerfully consider their lifetime value.

*Matthew 6:33-34 (NIV)*
*But seek first his kingdom and his righteousness, and all these things will be given to you as well. Therefore do not worry about tomorrow, for tomorrow will worry about itself. Each day has enough trouble of its own.*

**Being Present**
Failure or victory
Either way, the past
Steals from the present
This moment doesn't last.
Provision for tomorrow
Enough – a little more
We say the future justifies
Those voices we ignore.

We hear but do not listen
We see but do not know
We glimpse a connection

But too soon let it go.
To love is *being present*
Manifesting care
*Now*, is our moment –
That wedge of time we share.

*Bandit*

## 28

# Know the Truth

Self-delusion is a killer. Small dogs with big egos should look into the mirror every morning. That's what I tell my six-pound lap dog, Bandit. He becomes very aggressive upon meeting bigger dogs. He thinks he's tough and apparently has no concept of how quickly his neck could be snapped. He feels he's protecting me, and of course, I love him for it, but I still fear for his life.

Experience proves that an inaccurate self-concept usually takes one down a dangerous path. We act on what we think we know, so it's important to be correct. To look in the mirror and see too much or too little is a dangerous mistake.

## 2 Timothy 4:3 (NIV)

*For the time will come when people will not put up with sound doctrine. Instead, to suit their own desires, they will gather around them a great number of teachers to say what their itching ears want to hear.*

## Colossians 1:9-12 (NIV)

*For this reason, since the day we heard about you, we have not stopped praying for you. We continually ask God to fill you with the knowledge of his will through all the wisdom and understanding that the Spirit gives, so that you may live a life worthy of the Lord and please him in every way: bearing fruit in every good work, growing in the knowledge of God, being strengthened with all power according to his glorious might so that you may have great endurance and patience, and giving joyful thanks to the Father, who has qualified you to share in the inheritance of his holy people in the kingdom of light.*

## Time Out

Precious Father, thank You for not merely tossing me a mirror every morning, but rather inviting me to take Your hand and look upon Your face. When I seek to know You in the fullness of Your mercy and grace, then I come to know myself most accurately. Whether I am puffed up with pride or discouraged with sinful self, You alone lift me up and call me to a better place. You breathe strength and joy into my life, while holding me accountable to continuous character improvement. I praise and thank You for how carefully You love me. Amen.

## Today in-Christ

I will ask the Holy Spirit to speak His encouragement and truth to my heart and give me a self-concept wrapped in humility and truth.

*Psalms 27:4 (NIV)*
*One thing I ask from the* LORD, *this only do I seek: that I may dwell*
*in the house of the* LORD *all the days of my life, to gaze on the beauty*
*of the* LORD *and to seek him in his temple.*

**Know the Truth**
Mysteries of life we may not understand
Be not surprised but rather trust
Trust the Creator's hand.

With limited capacity
We make our judgments still
Only see in part ... as we exercise our will.
I put one foot ahead and follow with the other
Is it not the same for you
My sister and my brother?
But if I choose to never seek
His design and plan
I lose much joy in daily tasks
I have no one to surely ask
To lift me up on troubled days
No one bigger than me to praise.

Both logical and practical
My faith has become;
A platform of strength
For I am not the One
Who spins the stars and sun.

Spiritual authority- we naturally resist;
In prideful inferiority
We whine and cry and twist.
False sophistication
Eagerly fills our years

# RENEWAL

Grasp a bit of science to avoid our greatest fear
*We are never sovereign*
But accountable remain
To One beyond our limits
Who'll write the last refrain.

*Mom and Dad Carlson*

## 29

# Lesson One

While growing up with six brothers on the old farm, I didn't realize the pressures facing Mom and Dad. That's the way it should be. Our parents loved us dearly – no doubt of that. The farm provided a good life; not excessive but always enough. I recall the local grocery store owner Mr. Malmgren quietly telling Mom it was time to sell a steer because the bill was getting a little high. Get what you need, sign a slip, and walk out. It worked well.

Farm life back then wasn't so simple as much as it was simply good. For me, a twelve-year old, many serious lessons lay just ahead – but for now, just one.

I entered the living room and Mother explained that Auntie Gladys and Auntie Pearl had come to pray for her. It may have been a financial need or a health concern, or both. There was regularly a crisis to manage on the farm. Money was always short, the workload challenging. Often rocky ground lay between Mom and Dad.

God had become real to me at the age of ten. There in the living room, I shyly announced to the three sisters that I'd like to pray too. I was invited to do so. My prayer began with genuine concern, and after a few sentences, ended with absolute confidence that God would *deliver the goods*. I cannot recall many specifics, but I do know the essence of that moment because of the unfortunate incident that followed. Other than table prayers, this was my first attempt to pray aloud for an adult while in their presence. Apparently, one of my aunts had invited a visiting evangelist to join them in this prayer time for mother, but he had arrived a bit late. Standing silent behind me, he had heard my prayer. As he entered the room, he said, *"Now, we are really going to pray."* I am certain he didn't intend to hurt me. In our home, we knew how to be respectful to elders, so I'm sure my face did not reveal the pang of disappointment I felt. After a minute, I quietly left the room, probably unnoticed by everyone but Mom.

This was a valuable lesson for me. I learned that those who call themselves *Christian* do not always act in a *Christian* way. Surprisingly, my hurt wasn't comprised of self-pity, for as a child my faith was very strong. God had powerfully revealed Himself to me. I was familiar with the heart of God and His nature. I knew I had prayed a devout and valid prayer for Mother. Although this stranger had not validated it, I was confident that God had heard me. My distress was heavy because now I realized the *Christian* coin had two sides. Life became more complicated in that moment.

After 70 years of living, I too have had ample opportunity to join the universal ranks of those *saying Christian* but not always *doing Christian*. Still, this does not negate the reality, power and love of Jesus Christ. In spite of our sometimes poor examples, He remains the single greatest hope for our imperfect, selfish world.

## Time Out

Precious Redeemer, I praise You for Your faithfulness. In the midst of my inconsistency, Your character remains constant. Although we often misrepresent You, Father, You still whisper encouragement to us, reminding us that You are a God of second chances – always. Forgive me for those times when I have tarnished Your name by my selfish attitudes and actions. Amen.

## *Philippians 1:6 (NIV)*

*Being confident of this, that he who began a good work in you will carry it on to completion until the day of Christ Jesus.*

## Today in-Christ

I will not let my faith be shaken by the poor example of Christ's human ambassadors. Instead, I will fix my eyes on Jesus, the author and finisher of my faith, the only One consistently deserving of my praise.

**Lesson One**
A kind word said
But kind deed undone
Fair weather friend
No better than none
Oh where
Can I place my trust?

You say I should pray
And give God his due
Be faithful, stand strong-
But I'm looking at you
Oh where
Can I place my trust?

Only one reference point
Remains ever-true
Precious sweet Jesus
I'm looking at You.

*Canary Grass*

## 30

# Unto Us

She had a Lab puppy to give away and had responded to my classified ad. Eager to once again have canine companionship, I was hopeful – this may be the one. I drove to the woman's home via back country roads. In the -12° temp, I needed to convincingly talk myself into stopping for a quick shot of the tall, frosted, canary grass in the ditch – a bit of beauty amidst killing cold.

When she appeared at her door, she looked to be 75 years old, but instinctively, I felt she was probably less than 60. Had life's trials piled up high and poured over, causing wrinkles beyond her age? Apparently so.

I knew well what sort of pup I wanted; this one didn't qualify. She cried when I declined the dog, saying, though she loved the dog, it was too much for her now. *"I've had too many losses in my life. I can't manage or care for him like I should."*

I wanted to simply leave, but felt the Spirit tell me to ask about the source of her pain, which was obviously genuine and severe. She'd lost her 29-year-old son just a month ago. She pointed to a large portrait on the wall of her son – a handsome, healthy, athletic young man. She had also lost a sister and brother within the last nine months. Such great loss in a short amount of time.

Before opening the door and leaving, I offered to pray briefly and she readily accepted. *"Precious Father, we have no one but You, no other place to go but Jesus, to find healing and hope in times like these. Please send your Spirit's touch and Presence, to bring hope and some new light into this present darkness."* She sincerely thanked me, and I left.

As I stepped into the freezing cold, a voice sneered and mocked me: *"Look at you, attempting to pray to a God you have recently disobeyed. How meaningless! How empty! God no longer hears your pleas, your requests. Take a look at your enormous sin. Do you really believe a Holy God still desires to listen to you?"*

I backed out of the driveway, fully sensing the extreme despair of that broken woman – but felt I had failed; I doubted there was any credence to my prayer. I thought "the voice" was likely correct: *My days of caring for the needy stranger have certainly passed.* The weight of my sin and selfishness loomed large and powerful; it began to drown out my urge to pray for this person once again. But I did. *"Father, if this was the real reason You allowed me to meet her – simply so I might offer a 60-second prayer up to You on her behalf – then, PLEASE!, do in fact, touch her tonight with Your strength, healing and encouragement, that for which You inspired me to ask!"*

There was no feeling of victory – no assurance that my prayers had been or would be answered. But there was a small measure of trust ignited in my heart that perhaps God was still listening and active within me. Unaware of her grief when I first knocked on her door, it was certainly not my intention to pray with/for this woman. I know now that it was completely God's doing.

*Precious Father, through the power of Your love, grace and mercy, I continue to trust in renewal. When I look at my own righteousness or lack thereof, help me instead to focus my eyes on Christ. May I become evermore like You Jesus, gaining the capacity to diligently seek and rest in YOU. Help me, Lord, to never be too discouraged, too busy, or too laden with my own sin to share a God-inspired moment with someone more desperate than me. Amen.*

### Romans 8:35,37-39 AMP
*Who shall ever separate us from the love of Christ? Will tribulation, or distress, or persecution, or famine, or nakedness, or danger, or sword? Yet in all these things we are more than conquerors and gain an overwhelming victory through Him who loved us [so much that He died for us]. For I am convinced [and continue to be convinced—beyond any doubt] that neither death, nor life, nor angels, nor principalities, nor things present and threatening, nor things to come, nor powers, nor height, nor depth, nor any other created thing, will be able to separate us from the [unlimited] love of God, which is in Christ Jesus our Lord.*

### Isaiah 9:6 (KJV)
*For unto us a child is born, unto us a son is given: and the government shall be upon his shoulder: and his name shall be called Wonderful, Counselor, The mighty God, The everlasting Father, The Prince of Peace.*

**Unto Us**
Unto us He came
Restoring hope
Where only shame
Once lived and thrived.

The guilty one cries
*To whom can I go?*
*Who understands?*
*Or could possibly know*
*The weight of the burden*
*I bear?*

Laden with my sin
Christ answers my cry
*My life-blood given*
*For the sinner – I died*

So who will condemn
The prodigal child
Restored to the Father?
God answers
*Not I.*

*Robinson Park, Sandstone Quarry in Minnesota*

## 31

# Without Excuse

As I stood before the massive sandstone wall, many thoughts streamed through my head, each bearing an insight or question+, not of my own making. Spring water was seeping through cracks, causing the rock face to glisten in the light from the sun in the eastern sky. Water and Light – filling the voids and refreshing the faces of life. Ever persistent, water and light always find a means to bring dramatic transformation.

**Jeremiah 9:23-24 (NIV)**
*This is what the LORD says: "Let not the wise boast of their wisdom, or the strong boast of their strength or the rich boast of their riches, but let the one who boasts boast about this: that they have the*

understanding to know me, that I am the LORD, who exercises kindness, justice and righteousness on earth, for in these I delight," declares the LORD.

God is alive and relevant. Knowing Him is to grasp the utmost source of contentment, confidence and joy. Indeed, this is the supreme distinctive of the Christian faith: *in-Christ we come to know the Lord God personally.* His Spirit eagerly waits to show us His face in every corner of creation, in history, and in each new day.

### Romans 1:20 (NIV)

*For since the creation of the world God's invisible qualities—his eternal power and divine nature—have been clearly seen, being understood from what has been made, so that people are without excuse.*

Eternal goodness and blessing come only from trusting God and living in the awareness of His Presence. We may boast in our prideful capacities – we may even make our marks on stone, but earthly achievements are soon forgotten.

### Job 36:26-29 (NIV)

*How great is God – beyond our understanding! The number of his years is past finding out. He draws up the drops of water, which distill as rain to the streams; the clouds pour down their moisture and abundant showers fall on mankind. Who can understand how he spreads out the clouds, how he thunders from his pavilion?*

Today we may cling to many excuses for not seeking God: *I'm busy; there's much about Him I don't understand; I just don't have the faith needed; I'm okay where I'm at, I don't need Him right now.* Still, Christ is faithful. In the depth of our need, He asks, *"Shall I come and bring you My healing?"*

*Mathew 8: 5-8, 13 (NIV)*
*When Jesus had entered Capernaum, a centurion came to him,
asking for help. "Lord," he said, "my servant lies at home paralyzed,
suffering terribly." Jesus said to him, "Shall I come and heal him?"
The centurion replied, "Lord, I do not deserve to have you come
under my roof. But just say the word, and my servant will be
healed." Then Jesus said to the centurion, "Go! Let it be done just as
you believed it would." And his servant was healed at that moment.*

**Time Out**
Father I hear You calling "COME TO ME." Help me to let go of
pride and bring my remorse and repentance to You in simple faith.
Today as I consider the current troubles, I ask You, Jesus, to come
to me with the refreshment of Your Living Water and the Light of
Your Love. *COME into me JESUS. I ask for Your healing.* Amen.

**Without Excuse**
My habit is to see the walls
Read the signs that say to all
*No Hope Here.*

But God desiring intimacy
Tender familiarity
Brings His Spirit; offers faith

With cleansing Water Living
Glistening Light forgiving
His purpose is made known.

How can I refuse?
I am without excuse.
Love reaches out to me.

# For Individual Study

1. It is helpful to use a journal-sized notebook during your devotional time, capturing your thoughts and reflections as you read.

2. Read the devotional (one each day for 31 days).

3. Journal your thoughts, challenges and inspirations after reading the *Today in-Christ* section.

4. Journal your own personal prayer.

# For Group Discussion

1. Moderator may read the selection for today.

2. Ask: What are the key points that stood out or made an impression upon you?

3. Does the challenge as presented in *Today in-Christ* seem reasonable?

4. What other scripture verses or stories can you think of that bring insight to the subject?

5. What summary life principles may be taken away from today's reading?

Printed in the United States
by Baker & Taylor Publisher Services